Helping Children See Jesus

ISBN: 978-1-64104-028-0

God's King
Old Testament Volume 22: 2 Samuel

Author: Arlene S. Piepgrass
Illustrator: Vernon Henkel
Colorization Courtesy of Good Life Ministries
Page Layout: Patricia Pope

© 2021 Bible Visuals International
PO Box 153, Akron, PA 17501-0153
Phone: (717) 859-1131
www.biblevisuals.org

All rights reserved. No part of this publication may be reproduced, stored in a retrieval system or transmitted in any form by any means, electronic, mechanical, photocopy, recording or otherwise, without the prior permission of the publisher, except as provided by USA copyright law.

RELATED ITEMS

To access related items (such as activities, memory verse posters and translated texts) please visit our web store at www.biblevisuals.org and enter 2022 in the search box on the page.

FREE TEXT DOWNLOAD

To access a FREE printable copy of the teaching text (PDF format) in English or other available languages, enter 2022 in the search box. Add the item to your cart, and use coupon code XTACSV17 at checkout. Once your order is processed you will receive an email with a link to the free download.

STUDENT ACTIVITES

These are included with the FREE printable copy of the English teaching text for this story. See the directions under Free Text Download (above) to access them.

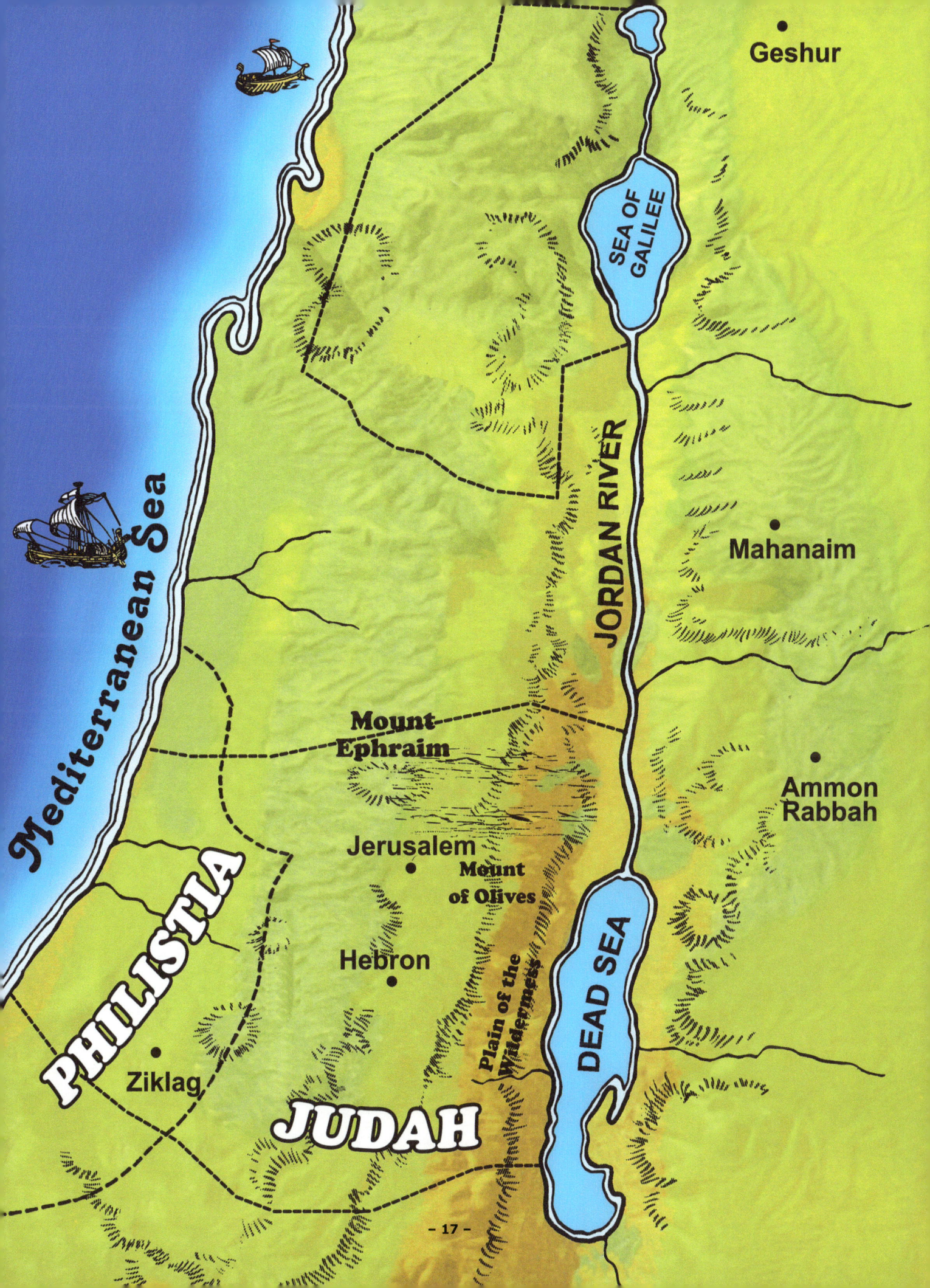

Trust in the LORD with all thine heart; and lean not unto thine own understanding. In all thy ways acknowledge Him, and He shall direct thy paths.

Proverbs 3:5, 6

Lesson 1
DAVID BECOMES KING OVER ISRAEL

NOTE TO THE TEACHER

Beginning with Abraham (Genesis 12) until Samuel's time, God was King of the Israelites. Then the Israelites wanted to be like the nations around them. They begged for an earthly king (1 Samuel 8). So God gave them what they wanted. He chose Saul as their king. If Saul had obeyed God, he would have had a wonderful reign. Instead, he willfully disobeyed. And God rejected him (1 Samuel 15:23-29).

In place of Saul, God chose David (1 Samuel 13:14). However, for many years Saul continued to rule over Israel.

David fought and won many battles for Saul. Then King Saul became jealous of David and tried to murder him. For years David spent his time running away form Saul. On two occasions David could have killed Saul. But David refused to touch the Lord's anointed king (1 Samuel 24 and 26). He waited for God to dethrone Saul and give it to him (David).

OBSERVE: These lessons should be taught following those in Volume 21. By using both volumes, the history of Israel and the life of David can be understood.

Scripture to be studied: 2 Samuel 1-9

The *aim* of the lesson: To show that God is on His throne in Heaven controlling everything.

What your students should *know*: That God sets up the kings and rulers of the earth (see Daniel 4:25b).

What your students should *feel*: Awe that God who has all power, cares about the details of our lives.

What your students should *do*: Allow God to lead them in their decisions and plans.

Lesson outline (for the teacher's and students' notebooks):
1. David's respect for Saul and love for Jonathan (2 Samuel 1).
2. Jerusalem becomes the capital of Israel (2 Samuel 5).
3. God's promise (covenant) (2 Samuel 7).
4. The King's compassion (2 Samuel 9).

The verses to be memorized:

Trust in the LORD with all thine heart; and lean not unto thine own understanding. In all thy ways acknowledge Him, and He shall direct thy paths. (Proverbs 3:5, 6)

THE LESSON

Have you ever had to wait long for a promised gift? (Let students share such experiences.) Did you think you would never receive the present? Did you decide the one who made the promise had forgotten?

1. DAVID'S RESPECT FOR SAUL AND LOVE FOR JONATHAN
2 Samuel 1

God told David he would be the next king of Israel. What was David doing when Samuel went to anoint him as king? (*Tending sheep*, 1 Samuel 16:11.) Who was king at that time? (*Saul.*) Why was God looking for a new king? (1 Samuel 13:14; 15:26.) (*Teacher:* Briefly review incidents which caused God to reject King Saul. 1 Samuel 13 and 15.)

Saul was jealous of David and hated him. For years he tried to kill David. Saul knew that one day David would replace him as king.

Indeed, so many people loved David. So many joined him that he had his own army. Often David and his men had to hide from King Saul. Sometimes they hid in caves. At other times they fled to Philistia. The Philistines were their neighbors–and their enemies.

David waited and waited to become king. But he never lost faith in God. He believed God would do what He had promised. Even when David had opportunities to slay Saul, he refused to touch him (1 Samuel 24:4-6; 26:8-10). David waited for God to give him the throne.

Waiting is hard. We like to know what is going to happen. We want it to happen quickly. God tells us He is "performing what He has planned for us" (Job 23:14). He works everything together for good. But He is not in a hurry.

(*Teacher:* Let students read aloud some of the following verses: Psalm 27:14; 37:7; 40:1; 46:10; 62:1, 5, 8; Isaiah 30:18; 40:31.)

When you get impatient and want things to happen quickly, remember David. God did not forget His promise. And He does not forget you.

David had reached age 30 (2 Samuel 5:4). He and his men were in the town of Ziklag. One day a man from Saul's army came running into town. His clothes were torn. He had dust on his head. These were signs that someone had died. The soldier fell at David's feet. David asked, "Where have you come from? What has happened?"

Show Illustration #1

"I have come from Saul's army," answered the man. "We have been defeated by the Philistines. Thousands of soldiers have been killed. King Saul and his son Jonathan are also dead. Here is the king's crown and one of his bracelets."

Do you think David was glad when he heard the news? (Let students give ideas.) Who would now be king? (*David.*)

In those days any new king murdered the entire family of the former king. Do you think David did that?

No! David did not give orders to kill Saul's family. Nor did he shout for joy. Instead, he and all his men were filled with sorrow. Sadly they tore their clothes, showing how grief-stricken they were. They wept all day for Saul and Jonathan.

Why did Jonathan's death make David sad? (Recall the friendship of David and Jonathan, 1 Samuel 18 and 20.) David would never again on earth see his good friend.

Why did David mourn for Saul–the one who tried to kill him? (*David respected Saul as God's designated king over Israel. Because David loved God, he forgave Saul.*) David wrote a beautiful song in memory of Saul and Jonathan. (Read 2 Samuel 1:24-27.)

2. JERUSALEM BECOMES THE CAPITAL OF ISRAEL
2 Samuel 5

Now David was the most important man in Israel. Who gave him this position? (*God.*) Would he forget God as Saul did?

How had God described David? (*A man after God's own heart*, 1 Samuel 13:14.) More than anything in the world, David wanted to please God.

Immediately David prayed to the LORD. "Shall I leave Ziklag and go to one of the cities in Judah?" he asked. (See 2 Samuel 2:1.)

"Yes, go up to Judah, David," answered the LORD.

"Where shall I go?" David asked.

"Go to the city of Hebron," the LORD said.

(*Teacher:* Review Proverbs 3:5-6 again. Apply to students.)

David, his family, and all his followers obediently moved to Hebron. There the men of Judah anointed him king.

But not all the Israelites accepted David as king. Some tried to make one of Saul's sons, Ishbosheth, king. Did they succeed? (*No.*) Why? (*Because God had rejected Saul's family. He had chosen David instead*, 1 Samuel 15:28.)

For seven years David ruled in Hebron over the province of Judah. He was waiting for God's time to reign over all the Israelites.

One day news spread throughout the country that Ishbosheth was dead. All the leaders of Israel came to David in Hebron. "We want you to be our king," they insisted. "When Saul was king, you led our armies. You are our brother. The Lord has said you should be our leader."

At last, David was crowned king over all the Israelites. God's promise to David was fulfilled! What a happy time that was! Everyone celebrated for three days! (See 1 Chronicles 12:23, 29, 40.)

As king, David took care of some important matters. First, David conquered Israel's enemies in and around Jerusalem. Next he moved from Hebron to Jerusalem. He called Jerusalem "the City of David." And he made it the *capital of Israel*.

Show Illustration #2

After that, King David had the Ark of God brought to Jerusalem. The Ark was to be kept in the Holiest Place of the Tabernacle. (Remind students that the Israelites worshiped God at the Tabernacle. God made His presence known above the Ark in the Holy of Holies.)

Let me tell you something which had happened many years before this. Some soldiers who disobeyed God, took the Ark of God into battle. (See 1 Samuel 4.) The Philistines captured the Ark and took it to their country. Because of this, God sent judgment to the Philistines for seven months. He punished them with boils, rats, and mice. Finally the Philistines returned the Ark to Israel. For 20 years it was kept in the home of one of the Israelites. Now King David placed the Ark in the Tabernacle. That is where it belonged. David made Jerusalem the *center of worship* for Israel. (Compare Deuteronomy 12:5.)

King David also built a beautiful palace (2 Samuel 5:11). He had lived in caves and moved from place to place for years. Now David was finally settled.

3. GOD'S PROMISE (COVENANT)
2 Samuel 7

David chose honest, God-loving men to be his advisors (Psalm 101:6). One of those men was Nathan. He was a prophet of God and a good friend to King David.

One day David said, "Nathan, I am living in this beautiful palace. But the Ark of God is in a tent. I would like to build a magnificent temple for the Lord."

"Do as you wish," replied Nathan. "The Lord is with you."

Do you think David's desire was good? (Let students respond.)

That very night God spoke to the prophet. "Nathan," the Lord said, "give this message to David. He is not to build a beautiful temple. It is good that he wants to do something for Me. Instead, *I* am going to do something greater for *him*."

The Lord told Nathan more. And Nathan took God's message to King David.

Show Illustration #3

Nathan began, "You were young when God chose you to lead His people. The Lord gave you and your army victory over your enemies. He has made your name great. God says He will make it even greater. He will give the Israelites *a land which will be theirs forever*. When you die, your son will build a temple for God. And he shall rule God's people. If he disobeys God, God will punish him. But the Lord will not remove him from the throne. David, *your kingly family line will last forever*."

This last promise was fulfilled hundreds of years later. The Lord Jesus Christ was born into the family of David's descendants (Matthew 1:1). When He returns to earth, He shall sit on the throne of David (Luke 1:32-33). Then the Lord Christ will rule the world (Revelation 11:15). No one knows when this will be.

Many years before David lived, God had promised to send One who will defeat Satan (Genesis 3:15). To David He renewed this promise. He explained that this One would come through David's family.

David listened to the message of God. Then he went into the Tabernacle and sat before the Lord. David worshiped God and praised Him for His wonderful promises. "Who am I, Lord, that You have bestowed such favor on me?" David prayed. "I am not important. My family is not important. How much You have done for me! How great You are, O Lord God! There is none like You. There is no other God beside You. Let Your name be magnified forever!"

4. THE KING'S COMPASSION
2 Samuel 9

King David often thought about his friend Jonathan, now dead. *I promised I would be kind to his family*, David remembered. He asked his servants, "Are any of Jonathan's children living?"

"Yes," they replied. "Prince Jonathan had a son named Mephibosheth. He is still living. When Saul was killed, his nurse fled with him. In her haste, she dropped him. He has been crippled–lame in both feet–ever since."

"Send for him immediately," David commanded.

When Mephibosheth received the king's order, he was troubled. He thought, *My grandfather, King Saul, hated David. He tried to kill David. Now King David is going to slay me in revenge. Kings always murder the families of their enemies.*

Mephibosheth was terrified when he was presented to King David. He fell on his face to honor the king.

Show Illustration #4

David spoke kindly to Mephibosheth. "Do not be afraid," the king said. "I am not going to harm you. I loved Jonathan your father very much. Because of him, I want to show kindness to you. I am returning to you all the land which belonged to your grandfather. Your grandfather's former servant, Ziba, and his sons will farm the land for you. But you will live with me in the palace. You shall eat at my table."

"Oh, King David! Why are you so kind to a dead dog like me?" Mephibosheth cried.

Mephibosheth had done nothing to deserve kindness from the king. He was honored because he was Jonathan's son.

David's kindness is a beautiful picture of God's love for us. God seeks us out. We are not worthy. We do not deserve His love. But for Christ's sake, God forgives those who trust in His Son (Ephesians 4:32).

Mephibosheth accepted King David's offer. He moved to the palace at Jerusalem. He feasted at the king's table.

Today God–the King over all kings–offers us salvation. He wants to save us from sin through His Son, Christ Jesus, who died for us. But we must accept His offer. Suppose Mephibosheth had refused the king's offer. Would he then have enjoyed the blessings of palace life? (*No.*)

You can refuse to accept the Lord Jesus Christ as your Saviour. By rejecting God's Son, you will be separated from Him forever. And for all eternity you will suffer punishment. So, this very day, place your trust in Jesus as your Saviour.

Lesson 2
KING DAVID SINS

Scripture to be studied: 2 Samuel 10-12

The *aim* of the lesson: To show that David, the man after God's own heart, was not perfect.

What your students should *know*: That God punishes sin but forgives the sinner who confesses his sin.

What your students should *feel*: Conviction of sin in their own lives.

What your students should *do*: Confess all known sin; accept God's forgiveness; seek to live in obedience to God's Word.

Lesson outline (for the teacher's and students' notebooks):

1. David's many wives (2 Samuel 5:13).
2. David and Bathsheba (2 Samuel 11:1-5).
3. David and Uriah (2 Samuel 11:6-27).
4. David and Nathan (2 Samuel 12:1-23).

The verses to be memorized:

Trust in the LORD with all thine heart; and lean not unto thine own understanding. In all thy ways acknowledge Him, and He shall direct thy paths. (Proverbs 3:5, 6)

NOTE TO THE TEACHER

For 20 years David ruled Israel well. He lived in fellowship with God. God gave him victories over his enemies. The Israelites prospered. The people loved David. David became one of the greatest spiritual leaders of the Old Testament.

King David was powerful and successful. Perhaps that is why he began to disobey God. David was not perfect. He did not always behave like a "man after God's own heart." But David did confess his sin and God forgave him. However, David suffered the punishment for his sin. This brought great sorrow to his life, his family, and his nation.

THE LESSON

Can you remember a time when you deliberately disobeyed your parents? How did you feel? Were you happy? Were your parents happy when they learned of your disobedience? Did they punish you? Why? Did they still love you? Did you tell them you were sorry? Did they forgive you?

Today we shall study one of the saddest events in the Bible. It is a lesson about sin. And sin is always distressing.

How was David described in the Bible? (*A man after God's own heart.*) Does that mean he was perfect? (*No.*) It means David loved God with all his heart. He really wanted to please God.

David was a good king, chosen by God. He had ruled the Israelites for 20 years. Everyone loved him. The Lord helped David defeat the enemies which surrounded Israel. So those bordering nations were afraid of him.

1. DAVID'S MANY WIVES
2 Samuel 5:13

Most of the time King David asked God to guide him. *Most of the time he obeyed God. But in one matter David disobeyed God. He had many wives.*

How many wives did God give to Adam? (*One.*) Later, God gave a law saying kings should not multiply wives. (Read aloud Deuteronomy 17:14-17.) King David ignored this law.

Show Illustration #5

When David moved from Hebron to Jerusalem, he took more wives. He did not ask God about this. Instead, he behaved like the pagan kings around Israel.

2. DAVID AND BATHSHEBA
2 Samuel 11:1-5

It was springtime. David's men were out of the city fighting against Israel's enemies. King David did not go out to battle with his army. He turned over the leadership to General Joab.

One evening David was strolling on his roof garden. Looking down, he saw a beautiful woman taking her bath.

Show Illustration #6

David called one of his servants. "Go see who that lovely woman is!" he commanded.

Soon the servant reported. "King David," he said, "that lady is Bathsheba.

– 21 –

Her husband is Uriah, one of your soldiers. He is in your army fighting under General Joab."

"Bring Bathsheba to my palace!" ordered David.

Do you think David had asked God about this? (*No.*) If he had, what would the Lord have told him? (Let students respond. Emphasize that this was sin.)

God's law commanded that no one should take another man's wife (Exodus 20:14). But King David was not thinking about the Lord. He was thinking only of himself. He wanted his own way. He was not happy without Bathsheba. So David's servant brought her to the palace.

The next morning Bathsheba went home. Life at the palace went on as usual. David hoped the servant wouldn't tell on him.

But Someone did not need to be told. The Lord God saw what King David had done. God's Word says, "Be sure your sin will find you out" (Numbers 32:23).

Weeks later David received a message from Bathsheba. It read, "King David, I am going to have a baby–your baby."

What shall I do? thought David. *The people dare not know what happened. Uriah must not learn about this.* David was trying to find a way to hide his sin. Previously, David had asked God to show him what to do. Why didn't he ask God this time? (*David knew he had sinned. He knew he'd displeased God.*)

3. DAVID AND URIAH
2 Samuel 11:6-27

David thought of a plan. He rushed a message to General Joab: "Send your soldier Uriah to the palace immediately."

Show Illustration #7

When Uriah arrived, the king acted as if everything was fine. "How are things going in the battle, Uriah?" he asked.

"The battle is going well," Uriah reported.

"That's good news," David responded. "Now, go home, Uriah. Spend the night there. You need a rest from fighting."

David was hoping to cover his sin. However, Uriah stayed at the palace door overnight.

King David learned about this in the morning. He asked, "Uriah, what is the matter with you? Why didn't you go home to your wife last night? You've been away fighting a long time."

"King David, I could not go home. I thought of all our soldiers and General Joab sleeping outside. Why should I rest at home when they are fighting for us?"

The king should have confessed his sin to the Lord. Instead he had another idea. He wrote a letter to General Joab and sealed it. The next morning he said to Uriah, "Return to your duty. And please give this letter to General Joab."

When Joab unsealed the king's letter, he read: "Put Uriah in the front line of the battle. Make sure that he will be killed!"

Think of that! King David was plotting the death of Uriah. He knew God's law. (Exodus 20:13.) But he ignored it. He deliberately disobeyed God.

Later a messenger arrived at the palace with news from General Joab. "We approached the city walls. Their strongest soldiers came out to fight us. Several of our soldiers–including Uriah–were killed."

What a relief! thought David. *Now I can bring Bathsheba to the palace as my wife. All will be well.*

Was everything well? Who saw all that had happened? (*The Lord God.*) Listen to what the Bible says. (Slowly read 2 Samuel 11:27–emphasizing the closing statement.)

4. DAVID AND NATHAN
2 Samuel 12:1-23

Several months went by. Then one day King David and all the Israelites rejoiced. A baby boy had been born in the palace.

But God was not pleased. He was grieved. His servant David had sinned. David the king had first lured Bathsheba to the palace. Then he had arranged for her husband, Uriah, to be slain.

Do you think David was really happy? No. He knew he had done wrong. He realized he had treated others unjustly. He knew he had disobeyed God. He tried to forget all this. But he could not. (Read Psalm 32:3-4.) No one can hurt others and be happy.

Why had God not stopped David from inviting Bathsheba to the palace? We do not know. But God gives us the freedom to make choices. (Read Joshua 24:15.) He longs for us to obey Him because we *want* to.

You will often be tempted to sin. But you can refuse to sin. The Lord will help you not to yield to temptation. (See 1 Corinthians 10:13.) But King David had ignored God. He wanted Bathsheba.

God, however, did not ignore David. One day He sent His prophet Nathan to the palace.

"King David, something wrong has happened in your kingdom," began Nathan.

"Tell me about it," said David with interest.

"Listen carefully," Nathan said. "There were two men in the city. One was rich and had many, many sheep and lambs. The other man was poor. He had only one little lamb. That lamb became his children's pet. It even drank from the poor man's cup and ate from his plate. How the family loved that one little lamb!"

Nathan continued, "One day the rich man had a guest. The rich man wanted to serve his guest a nice meal. He decided not to kill any of his own lambs for the feast. Instead he took the poor man's one little lamb. He killed it, roasted it, and served it to his guest!"

King David became wild with anger as he listened. "That man should be put to death!" he shouted. "He must give that poor man four lambs for the one he stole!"

Nathan looked David in the eye. Solemnly he said, "King David, *you* are that rich man!"

David was stunned. Nathan continued, "Listen to what the Lord God of Israel has spoken to you." (*Teacher:* Read aloud slowly 2 Samuel 12:7-9.)

God reminded David of all He had done for him. Then the Lord said, "You have despised My laws. You have done wickedly. Therefore you and your family will be punished. You acted secretly, David. But I shall punish you openly."

To Nathan David said, "I have sinned against the Lord!" King David was truly sorry. God saw the king's heart and knew he was sincere.

"Yes, David, you have sinned against God," replied Nathan. "But He forgives you. You will not die for your sins as you deserve. (See Leviticus 20:10.) You have brought great shame to the name of the Lord. You have given His enemies a reason to blaspheme Him. Because of this, your baby born to Bathsheba will die!"

Then Nathan left. And immediately David received word that his son was very sick.

Show Illustration #8

Falling down, David prayed. "O Lord God, please do not let the baby die." For seven days and nights David refused to eat. He continued to beg the Lord to save his son. On the seventh day, the child died.

David was broken-hearted because he had disobeyed God. He now took time to think. And he prayed–oh, how he prayed! (Have students read slowly parts of David's prayer in Psalm 51:1-3, 7b, 10, 12, 16.)

David was praying, "Dear God, have mercy on me. I have sinned greatly against You. You have the right to punish me any way You wish. I deserve it. You want me to be truthful and honest. But I have been sinful. Wash me and I shall be whiter than snow. Create in me a clean heart, O God. Put a right spirit within me. Restore Your perfect joy to me again. I could go to the Tabernacle and offer sacrifices for my sin. But that is not what You desire. You want me to be truly sorry for what I have done. I am sorry, dear Lord. Please forgive me. Then I shall tell others of Your forgiveness. I shall sing Your praises to everyone!"

Why could the Lord forgive the king?

1. David admitted his sin.
2. David was truly sorry for his sin.
3. David asked God to forgive him.

The Lord God still loved David and He forgave him. But he punished him.

How many times we are like David! We choose to do wrong. God says, "He that covereth his sins shall not prosper: but whoso confesseth and forsaketh them shall have mercy" (Proverbs 28:13).

David was a sinner. Although he loved God very much, he was not perfect. God recorded David's sin in the Bible to teach us some lessons. Let us list the truths we have learned.

1. We shall be tempted to sin. Immediately we must call on the Lord to help us say "no." (See James 4:7-8.)
2. Never try to cover sin. Confess it and ask God's forgiveness (1 John 1:9).
3. God sees us at all times (Job 34:21).
4. God hates sin (Romans 6:23a).
5. God loves His children, but He chastens them when they sin (Hebrews 12:6).

God says we are all sinners (Romans 3:23; 3:10). We all deserve eternal punishment. He sent His son, Jesus Christ, to die for our sins. The Lord Jesus rose from the grave. He offers you eternal life with Him in Heaven (John 11:25-26). You can have that life by receiving Christ as your Saviour. Will you do that right now?

Lesson 3
KING DAVID SUFFERS FOR HIS SINS

Scripture to be studied: 2 Samuel 13-18

The *aim* of the lesson: To show that God disciplines His children who deliberately sin.

What your students should *know*: That a person will reap what he sows.

What your students should *feel*: A desire to avoid sin.

What your students should *do*: Pray earnestly that they will not yield to temptation.

Lesson outline (for the teacher's and students' notebooks):

1. Amnon's immorality (2 Samuel 13:1-17).
2. Absalom's violence (2 Samuel 13:18-39).
3. Absalom's rebellion (2 Samuel 14:1-18:33).
4. David's remorse (2 Samuel 19:1-8).

The verses to be memorized:

Trust in the LORD with all thine heart; and lean not unto thine own understanding. In all thy ways acknowledge Him, and He shall direct thy paths. (Proverbs 3:5, 6)

THE LESSON

Have you ever planted flower seeds or vegetable seeds? (Let students tell what they have planted.) When you plant kernels of corn, what grows? (*Corn.*) Do you pick beans from a corn stalk? (*No, you reap what you plant.*)

A verse in the Bible says: "Be not deceived; God is not mocked: for whatsoever a man sows, that shall he also reap" (Galatians 6:7). This verse is not speaking of seed-planting. It is talking about what we *do* each day. If we constantly do wrong, we shall suffer the consequences. By deliberately disobeying those in authority over you, you'll have trouble. That is the consequence of your disobedience. Good parents discipline their children because they love them. They want to help them learn what is right and wrong.

> **NOTE TO THE TEACHER**
>
> God promises, "If we confess our sins, He is faithful and just to forgive us our sins and to cleanse us from all unrighteousness" (1 John 1:9). The Lord warns, "Be not deceived; God is not mocked: for whatsoever a man soweth, that shall he also reap" (Galatians 6:7).
>
> God is a loving Father who disciplines His sinning children. (See Hebrews 12:5-8.) The Lord immediately forgave David when he confessed his sins. (2 Samuel 12:13). But David's wrong-doing affected his family and his nation. Anyone who sins has a bad affect on the lives of others.
>
> David experienced the chastening of a loving heavenly Father. He did not receive the judgment of the holy God (Hebrews 12:6).

God loves us. He wants us to obey Him. Obedience to the Lord brings us joy and happiness.

God loved David and King David loved God. But what did David do that displeased the Lord? (*He took another man's wife and arranged for her husband to be killed.*) Did God forgive David? (*Yes.*) David continued to be king. He had been chosen by God. But Nathan gave him a warning. "David, your sin will bring trouble to you and your family." This trouble would be the result of David's sin.

1. AMNON'S IMMORALITY
2 Samuel 13:1-17

Do you remember that King David had many wives? Was there anything wrong with that? (*God's plan was for man and woman to be one*, Genesis 2:24.)

One of David's wives had a son named Amnon (2 Samuel 3:2). With another wife, David had a daughter named Tamar. Tamar was a beautiful young girl. Amnon fell in love with her. He wanted to go to bed with her without their being married. But this is forbidden by God. Therefore, it is sin.

Day after day Amnon watched Tamar. Every day he was miserable because he could not have her. Amnon became exceedingly down-hearted. His friend Jonadab was concerned for him.

Show Illustration #9

Jonadab asked, "Amnon, what is the matter with you? You are sad all the time. Tell me what is troubling you."

"I am in love with my half-sister, Tamar," replied Amnon.

"The king's son should have anything he wants!" Jonadab exclaimed. "Let me tell you what to do. Pretend you are sick. Ask your father, King David, to send Tamar to your room to prepare food for you. Tell him you will feel better if she does this."

Amnon liked Jonadab's idea. So it was that Tamar prepared a nice meal for Amnon. Instead of eating, Amnon forced Tamar to lie down with him.

When David heard what Amnon had done, he was furious. He knew the Word of God. (See Leviticus 20:17.) But he did not punish Amnon.

Was Jonadab really a good friend? (Take time for discussion. Emphasize: *Jonadab encouraged Amnon to lie; to sin against Tamar; to disobey God's law*. God forbids marriage relationship with one's half-sister. See Leviticus 18:11.)

What should you do when friends urge you to do wrong? (*Do not listen to them; refuse to participate.*) Beware of being like Jonadab. Never, never encourage your friends to sin!

2. ABSALOM'S VIOLENCE
2 Samuel 13:18-39

Tamar had another brother named Absalom. He saw Tamar sobbing. He asked, "Did Amnon force you to lie down with him?"

Tamar nodded her head.

Immediately Absalom hated Amnon. *I shall get revenge,* he thought. *My father did not punish him. But he will not get away with his sin against my sister.*

Two years went by. Then one day Absalom went to King David. "It is sheepshearing time," he said. "I am planning a big party to celebrate. Will you and all your sons come?"

"No, my son," David answered. "If all of us came it would be too expensive for you."

"If you cannot come, Father, send Amnon in your place," urged Absalom.

King David agreed, So all his sons attended the celebration.

Meanwhile Absalom plotted against Amnon. He called some of his men to him. "When I give you the signal," he whispered, "kill Amnon."

So Absalom's party turned to horror.

Show Illustration #10

Amnon was murdered. All the other brothers fled on their mules. To save his own life, Absalom hid in the land of Geshur.

David was broken-hearted when he heard what had happened. The words of Nathan were really coming true: "Your sin will bring trouble to you and your family." Absalom's wicked deed reminded David of his responsibility for Uriah's death. Could he, being guilty, punish his son for murder? He should have. A father needs to teach his son to do right.

3. ABSALOM'S REBELLION
2 Samuel 14:1-18:33

Three years went by. Absalom stayed in Geshur. He was afraid to return to the palace. He knew he deserved death for what he had done.

One day Joab, King David's general, took a message to Absalom. "Your father misses you, Absalom," he said. "He wants you to return to Jerusalem."

"Good!" Absalom exclaimed. "Then he has forgiven me."

"Well, he has not entirely forgiven you. He says you cannot live at the palace. And you cannot see him," said Joab. So Absalom returned to Jerusalem. But he did not see his father. Nor could he live with him.

Two years went by. King David finally invited Absalom to live at the palace.

From then on, Absalom tried to turn people against the king. Think of that! Absalom was handsome–the most handsome young man in Israel. He had long, beautiful hair of which he was very proud. With his charm, Absalom won the hearts of men and women. More than anything else, Absalom wanted to become king. Was that a good ambition for him? (*No. God had chosen David as king.*)

Show Illustration #11

Day after day Absalom stayed at the city gates. When people came to see King David, Absalom stopped them. "Where do you come from?" he asked. "What is your problem?"

He listened to their difficulties. Then he would say, "My father is too busy to help you. If I were king, I could help *you*. I would treat you justly. I would give you your rights. But I am not the king. How I wish I could help you!"

Absalom would then shake their hands and kiss them. People were flattered by this handsome prince. Soon they were saying, "Maybe we should make Absalom king."

This is exactly what Absalom wanted to hear. In time, he was certain that enough people sided with him. So he made plans to overthrow King David. Think of it! Absalom plotted to kill his own father and take the throne! Do you think he talked to God about his plans? (*No. There is no verse that says Absalom ever prayed to God.*)

In time, David learned what Absalom planned to do. Surely King David recalled the words of the prophet. "Your sin will bring trouble to you and to your family." The prophet Nathan's words were true.

The king and his followers fled from Jerusalem. Absalom and his men took over the city. Soon civil war started. Father and son fought against each other. David's heart was broken. He didn't want such a battle. He wept. And those who loved him wept with him.

David now talked to his best Friend. Who was that? (*God.*) David loved God and God loved David, the king. Did the Lord hear David's prayer? Listen!

Absalom went to two of his men for advice. Each gave him different ideas for attacking King David. Absalom pondered which man's counsel was better. At last his mind was made up. So he launched his attack against David and his men. But he lost the battle and also his life (2 Samuel 18:14-15). The Lord had caused Absalom to follow the wrong advice. God is always in control. He who is Lord over all controls hearts, minds, and decisions.

4. DAVID'S REMORSE
2 Samuel 19:1-8

ABSALOM IS DEAD! ABSALOM IS DEAD! How do *you* suppose David felt when he heard this news? (Encourage student discussion.) Although Absalom had rebelled against his father, David still loved him. The king didn't like what Absalom had done. But Absalom was his son.

Show Illustration #12

With a broken heart, King David went to his room alone. "O my son Absalom, my son, my son Absalom!" he cried. "If only I could have died instead of you!" David was reaping the consequences of his sin. Again God had struck David's family.

After Absalom's death, King David returned to Jerusalem to rule. Those who had opposed him, again became loyal to him.

What lessons have you learned from these incidents in David's life?

1. As God's children, we should fear sin. God does not close His eyes to sin. As a loving Father, He punishes sin.
2. Do not listen to friends who tempt you to do wrong.
3. Do not tempt others to sin.
4. Be sure your ambitions are pleasing to God.
5. Whatever you sow, you will reap (Galatians 6:7).
6. You hurt others when you sin.

How can we keep from living sinfully?

1. Study God's Word and obey it.
2. Pray about everything.
3. Let the Holy Spirit guide you each day.
4. Discuss your activities and plans with Bible-loving Christian leaders.

Lesson 4
KING DAVID IS SENSITIVE TO GOD

NOTE TO THE TEACHER

In concluding this series, review the highlights of David's life.

Emphasize God's testimony of David—"a man after God's own heart." This does not mean David was perfect. But he truly loved the Lord and wanted to please Him. Even so, at times he failed to trust God. Always he confessed his sin to the Lord and asked forgiveness. The Lord knew that David really wanted to do God's will (Acts 13:22). Thus he was a "man after God's own heart" (1 Samuel 13:14; see 16:7).

David's life is an encouragement to us. When we do wrong, we must confess our sin to God. Then, if we are truly sincere, He will pardon us. But we should earnestly do our best never to do wrong.

You may have to explain the meaning of a "threshing floor." It is a place where, by pounding, seeds are separated from husks or straw.

Scripture to be studied: 2 Samuel 21-24; 1 Chronicles 21-22, 28-29

The *aim* of the lesson: To show that God, King over all, is merciful and kind.

What your students should *know*: That God requires His servants to honor and obey Him.

What your students should *feel*: Reverence for our great God.

What your students should *do*: Praise God for His love and mercy.

Lesson outline (for the teacher's and students' notebooks):

1. King David numbers Israel (2 Samuel 24:1-9; 1 Chronicles 21:1-7).
2. King David repents and worships (2 Samuel 24:1-25; 1 Chronicles 21:8-30).
3. King David submits to God's will (1 Chronicles 22:1-19; 28:1-21).
4. King David glorifies God (2 Samuel 22:1-51).

The verses to be memorized:

Trust in the LORD with all thine heart; and lean not unto thine own understanding. In all thy ways acknowledge Him, and He shall direct thy paths. (Proverbs 3:5, 6)

THE LESSON

Is there anyone here today who is perfect . . . one who has NEVER done anything wrong? (*No!*) Only one Person who ever lived on earth was perfect. Who was that? (*The Lord Jesus Christ*)

How did God describe David? (*A man after God's own heart.*) Did this mean he was perfect? (*No*) How do we know he was not perfect? (*God recorded in His Word the sins of David.*) Did the Lord no longer love David? Was David no longer a man after God's own heart? Each time David truly confessed his sin, God forgave him. David really wanted to honor the Lord and please Him. Because of this he continued to be "a man after God's own heart."

1. KING DAVID NUMBERS ISRAEL
2 Samuel 24:1-9; 1 Chronicles 21:1-7

After Absalom died, King David returned to Jerusalem. Again he sat on the throne. Once more peace was established throughout the land of Israel. It would be nice to say, "Thereafter David always pleased God." But that would not be the truth.

One day David called General Joab to the palace. "Count every person in Israel," the king commanded. "Find out how many men can go to war."

– 25 –

"Why do you want to do that?" questioned General Joab. "All the Israelite people are yours. Why must you know how many there are? Are you proud of *your* strength?"

"Do as I say!" commanded the king.

Show Illustration #13

General Joab and his military officers obeyed. For almost ten months they went to every town throughout Israel. One by one, each person registered. Finally, all the people were counted.

The Lord had not told David to do this. David had not asked God if this plan was pleasing to Him. The Lord looked inside David's heart. He saw that David was not trusting the power of God. He trusted in the size of his army. The Lord God was not pleased.

2. KING DAVID REPENTS AND WORSHIPS
2 Samuel 24:1-25; 1 Chronicles 21:8-30

Months later, General Joab brought his report to the king. Suddenly David realized he had sinned. "Why did I do this?" he asked the Lord. "I have been proud. I have been relying on the strength of my army. I have not trusted in You, God. Please forgive me. I have acted very foolishly."

The Lord did forgive David. But again the consequences of his sin hurt others.

God sent a prophet named Gad with a message. "King David, God is going to discipline you for your sin." Gad continued, "This time you may choose your punishment: (1) You will have *seven years* of famine in the land. Or, (2) You can flee from your enemies for *three months*. Or, (3) God will send *three days* of pestilence to the land. [Explain that *pestilence* is a contagious epidemic disease.] Think about it and choose one."

What a hard decision David had to make!

Finally King David made up his mind. He went to the Prophet Gad. "Let us fall into the hand of the Lord," he said. "His mercies are great. Do not let me fall into the hand of man. I choose three days of pestilence in the land."

So the Lord sent pestilence. One day, two days, three days, people died. David was heartbroken. He cried, "O God, I'm the one who sinned. I'm the guilty one. These people have done no wrong. Please punish me and my family but spare my people."

God sent another message to King David through His prophet. "Go, build an altar on the threshing floor of the man named Araunah." King David knew what had happened there many years before. That was the place where Abraham had offered his son Isaac. (Briefly review the incident from Genesis 22.) Immediately King David obeyed the Lord.

Araunah saw King David and his servants approaching. Frightened, Araunah bowed before the king. "Why has my lord the king come to me?" he asked.

"I want to buy your threshing floor. On it I shall build an altar to the Lord God. Then He will stop the pestilence in our land," David explained.

"O king, I shall *give* it to you. You may take my oxen for your sacrifice. Take the threshing tools. Use the ox yokes for fire under the sacrifice. All is yours. You need not pay for anything," Araunah insisted.

Show Illustration #14

Listen to the king's reply. "No, Araunah. I shall not take all this as a gift. I shall pay for it. I shall not sacrifice to the Lord God burnt offerings which cost me nothing."

David paid for everything and offered the sacrifices God commanded. God looked inside David's heart. He saw that the king was truly sorry for his sin. The Lord was pleased. He forgave David and stopped the pestilence. But 70,000 men lay dead.

3. KING DAVID SUBMITS TO GOD'S WILL
1 Chronicles 22:1-19; 28:1-21

The time came when David wanted to build a magnificent temple for God. But the Lord said, "No, David. You have fought many battles and caused much bloodshed. You shall not build My Temple. Rather, your son, Solomon, will build a house for My name" (1 Chronicles 22:8-10).

Show Illustration #15

David could have become angry because God refused his wish. Instead, he made plans for the construction of the Temple. He gathered the materials Solomon would need for the building. He commanded the leaders of Israel to help Solomon. He chose skillful men to do the work. (See 1 Chronicles 22.)

Where do you think the Temple of God was to be built? Right on the property David had purchased from Araunah. So David paid for the site of the Temple. He bought it with his own money. But he was not allowed to build God's Temple.

David was not angry because he could not have his own way. He did not become jealous of Solomon. He obeyed God completely. The king was glad for the privilege Solomon would have. Listen to King David's advice to his son, Solomon. (Read slowly 1 Chronicles 28:9.) That is good advice for each one of us.

4. KING DAVID GLORIFIES GOD
2 Samuel 22:1-51

During his lifetime, David wrote songs about God. The Bible book of the Psalms contains many of these songs. Two other songs of David's appear at the end of 2 Samuel. David often played these songs on his harp.

Show Illustration #16

In one song, David calls God his rock, his fortress, his refuge (2 Samuel 22:2-3). What did he mean? (*The Lord is strong; those who trust Him are safe.*)

He speaks of God as the One who saves from violence (2 Samuel 22:3). He delivers from danger (2 Samuel 22:18). What does that tell us? (*God is powerful, protective, caring.*)

God rewarded David when he was obedient. (See 2 Samuel 22:21, 25.) (*God is gracious.*)

God guided David (2 Samuel 22:29). (*God gives us wisdom also.* See James 1:5.)

David really wanted to do the will of God. Often, however, he did wrong. Whenever he failed, he was truly sorry and repented. He asked God's forgiveness. He prayed that God would give him right attitudes about everything. Above all else, David wanted the Lord God to be honored.

David was *God's* king. The Lord chose him to reign on the throne of Israel. God gave him victories over his enemies. The Lord God punished David when he sinned. God protected King David when others wanted to destroy him. The Lord used David to accomplish His purposes.

Many years later, long after David died, God wonderfully honored him. The Lord Jesus was born to one of David's descendants. (See upper right of illustration #16.) The New Testament speaks of Christ as "the Son of David" (Matthew 1:6; 9:27; 22:42).

Today the Lord God is our King. He is Ruler of all the universe. He has put you and me in this place. He wants us–as He wanted David–to obey Him. He has a plan for you and for me. Above all else, He wants us to praise Him and honor Him.

God wants each Christian to be a person "after His own heart." How can we do this? (*By obeying those in authority over us. By telling others that the Lord Jesus died for them. By singing songs which honor the Lord. By saying "no" when we are tempted to do wrong.*)

How can an unbeliever be a person after God's own heart? (*Believe in Christ and receive Him as your personal Saviour.*) Then He will give you a heart that *wants* to please God. You cannot please Him by yourself. You will not be perfect. But you will *want* to please the Lord. And if you yield to Him, He will help you always.